FUNNY PAPERS

FUNNY PAPERS
BEHIND THE SCENES OF THE COMICS

WRITTEN BY
ELAINE SCOTT

PHOTOGRAPHS BY
MARGARET MILLER

MORROW JUNIOR BOOKS   NEW YORK

To my sister, Kathy, with love and thanks for always making me laugh   —E. S.

ACKNOWLEDGMENTS

No writer ever produces a book alone. It takes many people, working together, to turn a stack of typewritten pages—my manuscript—into the book you are holding in your hands. I could not have written this book without the help of the wonderful cartoonists who willingly took time from their busy hours at the drawing board to share their stories with me. So, my warmest thanks go to Chance Browne, Chris Browne, Mort Gerberg, Hank Ketcham, John Cullen Murphy, Mike Peters, Bill Rechin, Charles Schulz, Brian Walker, Greg Walker, Mort Walker, and Don Wilder.

Many, many thanks also to Ted Hannah and Paul Hendricks of King Features Syndicate, Sarah Gillespie, Jeanne De Simone, and Diane Reed of United Feature Syndicate, Michael Hobson and John Romita from Marvel Comics, Lauren Bresnan of Sotheby's, Lucy Shelton Caswell from Ohio State University, and Ernie Williamson of the *Houston Post*.

Printing the Sunday funnies is a complicated and serious business, and I thank Tim Rosenthal and Jim Kraws of American Color for their patient explanations and exciting tour of the plant. Mrs. Moya Mischon's sixth-grade language arts students at Killough Middle School in Houston, Texas, helped by writing about their favorite comics. My young friend Matthew Christopher Jones provided excellent and helpful written comments, which I appreciate very much. And of course, I thank everyone at Morrow Junior Books, but especially my editor, Kitty Flynn, who worked alongside me every step of the way.

ART AND PHOTO CREDITS

The Publisher wishes to thank the syndicates for permission to reprint the cartoons and comic strips. Permission to reproduce other artwork is gratefully acknowledged: reproduced courtesy of General Research Division, New York Public Library, Aftor, Lenox and Tilden Foundations, pp. 20, 24; © 1993 by David Small, p. 26; first appeared in *Working Mother*, November 1991, printed with permission of *Working Mother* magazine, copyright © 1991 by WWT Partnership, Inc., p. 17. Permission to reproduce photographs, other than those by Margaret Miller, is gratefully acknowledged: The Bettmann Archive, pp. 64, 76; David Crommie, p. 40; © 1993 Marvel Entertainment Group, Inc., all rights reserved, p. 77; Jeannie Schulz, p. 13. Spider-Man appears on the jacket courtesy of Marvel Entertainment Group, Inc., all rights reserved.

Printed in the United States of America.   1 2 3 4 5 6 7 8 9 10
Library of Congress Cataloging-in-Publication Data
Scott, Elaine.   Funny papers : behind the scenes of the comics / by Elaine Scott ; photographs by Margaret Miller. p. cm. Includes index. Summary: Surveys the history of comic strips, examines different kinds and examples, and discusses how they are created and marketed.   ISBN 0-688-11575-6 (trade).—ISBN 0-688-11576-4 (lib. bdg.)   1. Comic books, strips, etc.—United States—Juvenile literature. [1. Cartoons and comics.]   I. Miller, Margaret, ill. II. Title. PN6725.S53 1993 741.5'0973—dc20 92-46727 CIP AC

6758

CONTENTS

INTRODUCTION

Do you read the comics? If you do, you are part of the 100 million Americans of all ages who read about the adventures of favorite characters in *Blondie, Peanuts, Garfield, Calvin and Hobbes, Beetle Bailey, Hi and Lois, Hagar the Horrible, Prince Valiant, Dennis the Menace, Mother Goose & Grimm,* and dozens of other comics every day. You are joined in this pastime by millions of other people in countries that circle the globe. American comic strips and cartoons are translated into sixty languages and appear in thousands of newspapers from New Zealand to New York. *Funny papers, funnies, comics*—these are all words for a kind of literature that is a genuine American art form. Only a few art forms actually began in the United States. Among them are jazz, music that was originated by African-Americans living in the South; quilting, a kind of sewing made

Garfield reprinted by permission of UFS, Inc.

popular by American women in the early days of this country (and now enjoyed by many men); and the comics, a combination of words and funny pictures that was born almost one hundred years ago on May 5, 1895.

On that date, Richard Outcault created a cartoon—or panel, as cartoonists call it—for the Sunday edition of the *New York World*. The panel featured a young boy with an oversize head and very large ears who was always dressed in a yellow nightshirt. The nameless boy and his friends lived and played in a place called Hogan's Alley, a run-down area of a large city that Outcault never identified. The artist called his cartoon *At the Circus in Hogan's Alley*, and it ran every Sunday in the *New York World*, a newspaper owned by Joseph Pulitzer. In those days long before television or movies, the Yellow Kid, as the character came to be known, caught the imagination of the public. Every Sunday the sales of the *World* jumped, as more and more people bought the paper to read about the Yellow

Kid's adventures with his friends.

Now the *World* was not the only newspaper published in New York City at that time. Among its competitors was William Randolph Hearst's *New York Journal*. Hearst noticed the increase in Sunday sales of the *World* and quickly figured out why it was happening—people were buying the paper in order to read about the Yellow Kid. Mr. Hearst wanted that cartoon for the *Journal* so the sales of his paper would increase, too. He decided to hire Outcault away from the *New York World*. Richard Outcault accepted Mr. Hearst's offer and began to draw his comic for the *New York Journal*.

Naturally, the *New York World* didn't want to lose its readers—or its new comic—so Mr. Pulitzer hired someone else to continue to draw *The Yellow Kid*, as the strip had come to be called, for his paper. A battle between the two newspapers began, and for a while *The Yellow Kid* appeared in both the *World* and the *Journal*. The competition between the papers became fierce and resulted in a term, *yellow journalism*, that is still used today to describe newspapers that resort to competitive (and sometimes questionable) methods to attract readers and increase their sales.

Although *The Yellow Kid* began its life as a single panel, within a year Richard Outcault began to tell his stories in a series of panels, and the comic strip was born. Soon other artists were drawing comic strips. New strips and new characters appeared—but only on Sunday, and Sunday newspaper sales soared. Everyone loved the funny papers.

During this time, the very beginning of the twentieth century, many hundreds of thousands of immigrants were

The Yellow Kid
© King Features Syndicate, Inc. Reprinted by special permission.

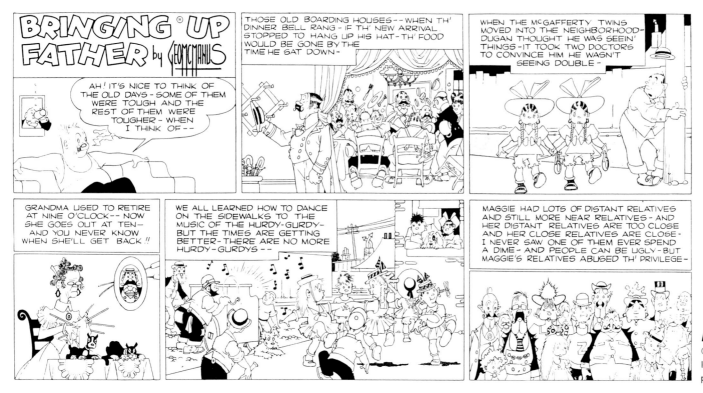

Bringing Up Father
© King Features Syndicate, Inc. Reprinted by special permission.

coming to the United States in search of a better future. The new Americans were a mix of people from different countries, and the comics reflected that mix. Though no one was certain what nationality the Yellow Kid and his friends were, they were obviously immigrants. So were other popular comic characters of the time, such as the Katzenjammer Kids, who were German, and Maggie and Jiggs in the popular strip _Bringing Up Father_, who were Irish.

The funny papers featured stories about America's new immigrants, and they also began to copy forms of American entertainment, such as vaudeville. Vaudeville was a kind of stage show performed in local theaters. In addition to skits, songs, and dances, every vaudeville show had a two-person comedy team who stood up and traded jokes with each other.

Before long, the comic strips included vaudeville-like material, too. Bud Fisher created two characters who exchanged snappy dialogue, similar to that of a vaudeville comedy team. Their names were Mutt and Jeff. In 1907,

Mutt and Jeff became the first comic strip to appear in newspapers on a daily basis.

With the beginning of daily strips, more and more comic characters appeared on the scene. Some, like the Yellow Kid, lasted for a while, then faded away. Strips about other characters—Li'l Abner, for example—stopped when the cartoonist who created them died. But other strips, like *Blondie*, became American institutions whose stories continue to this day, long after their original creators have retired or died.

From the lives of immigrants to the imagination of a little boy and his stuffed tiger, through words and pictures, the comics have always given Americans something in common—reading material that appears everywhere across the country at the same time. Reading the daily comics, like going to the movies or voting in a national election, unites Americans in a common experience.

In the *Calvin and Hobbes* strip by Bill Watterson that appears on the next page, young Calvin has sensed the significance of having something in common with other

people around the country. In this case, he wants cable TV, and he argues for it by saying that watching the same television shows helps keep everyone in our culture homogeneous. When something is homogenized, all of the particles are blended together so that nothing is distinct or different. Cream does not rise to the top in homogenized milk because the fat particles are blended into the milk and seem to disappear. Anyone who read *Calvin and Hobbes* on August 29, 1992, could get a good discussion going about whether having everything the same in a society is a good or bad thing.

So the comics may make us think about social issues, teach us something, or make us mad, but most often they make us smile—and perhaps even laugh out loud.

Unfortunately, things that make us laugh, though they are very popular, are not always treated with as much respect as work on a more serious topic. A funny book is often called "light" reading, as if "heavy" reading (whatever that is) was somehow better. The walls of the country's largest museums are hung with paintings called fine art, but you rarely see the original art for a comic strip hanging there. And yet the comics are an important part of American culture.

The comics can make us laugh, and laughter is a wonderful thing. The artists and writers who cause us to laugh at ourselves, our mistakes, and our prejudices contribute to our understanding of ourselves and one another. Reading the comics brings people together, keeps us informed and entertained, and helps us communicate with one another on a variety of timely and important topics. Furthermore, since American comic strips appear in newspapers all over the world, they help people from different cultures understand what we Americans are laughing at and thinking about. The comics deserve our attention and respect; reading comics and comic books, like any other kind of reading, is a worthwhile activity. This book will show you how this uniquely American art form is created and shared with readers everywhere.

Curling up with comic books is a good way to spend an afternoon.

JOKES, GAGS, AND STORIES

When the daily newspaper arrives in homes across America, the section many people turn to first is the comics. One business executive says, "I read the funny pages first because I need a laugh before I read the bad news in the rest of the paper!" The truth is, whether they are read first or last, more people read the comic pages than the sports, financial, or editorial sections. In fact, there are people who pay little attention to the news in the rest of the paper—they buy it to read the comics.

Today's comic pages contain a mix of cartoons and comic strips, and perhaps a puzzle or two. Some people read every single word of every strip and cartoon, but others follow just a few favorites. Nevertheless, there is probably no single item that is clipped, photocopied, mailed, or stuck on bulletin boards and refrigerators more than America's cartoons and comic strips.

Although cartoons and comic strips appear to be similar, they are actually two different forms of the same art. And each form requires a different kind of thinking on the part of the cartoonist who creates it.

A cartoon, or panel, is really a visual joke. In one drawing and a very few—or even no—words, the cartoonist must instantly communicate a funny idea. As the reader, you have to "get it" the minute you see it. The cartoonist doesn't have time to explain the characters, who they are and what they are doing. And the cartoonist cannot take time to explain the setting, either. The reader has to understand where the scene is set as soon as he or she looks at the panel. Therefore, the situations and the scenes that

Snafu
reprinted by permission of NEA, Inc.

"This is gonna be worse than I thought."

are drawn in most cartoons are familiar ones—children in school, families at home, people at work or visiting in their neighborhoods. The cartoonist's talent lies in taking one of the common situations that we all share and making us laugh about something in it.

However, no one knows exactly what will make another person laugh. A joke is a kind of mystery, and our ideas of what is funny change as we grow and change. Most of us laugh at things that used to frighten us. Perhaps we are laughing because we are relieved that we aren't frightened anymore! Thousands of students have been sent to the principal's office, so it is a familiar experience to most readers. Cartoonist Bruce Beattie has taken this experience, exaggerated it to make it appear far worse than it is, and turned the whole moment into a joke.

Dennis the Menace
© North America Syndicate, Inc. Reprinted by special permission.

"CARTOONS ARE LIKE CANDY FOR THE EYES."

10

Hank Ketcham uses every inch of space in his panel.

recall doing the same things in their own families."

So we see that a cartoon can make us laugh because there is something unexpected in it, like Dennis's statement that animated cartoons are like candy for the eyes, or it can be funny because we recognize something familiar in the panel, like the crying little brother in *The Family Circus*, or it can amuse us because we realize, as we look at the *Snafu* cartoon by Bruce Beattie, that school principals do not chop off students' heads, no matter how badly they behave!

One of America's best-loved comic strips had its beginnings as a panel called *Li'l Folks*, which appeared in the *St. Paul Pioneer Press* in St. Paul, Minnesota. In 1950, the

Although no one knows exactly what will make another person laugh, cartoonists each have their own ideas. Hank Ketcham, who draws *Dennis the Menace*, says, "The perfect cartoon has to be a marriage of picture and words, a kind of tepee where one depends on the other. The panel should have a funny, attractive picture with a caption that comes as a surprise. A big part of humor is the unexpected."

On the other hand, Bil Keane, who draws *The Family Circus*, has a different view about the humor in his panel. "I don't try to make my cartoons especially funny," he says. "I would rather have the readers react with a warm smile, a tug at the heart, or a lump in the throat as they

The Family Circus © Cowles Syndicate, Inc. Reprinted by special permission.

"Your little brother looks a lot like my little brother."

11

Peanuts
reprinted by permission of
UFS, Inc.

young cartoonist, whose nickname was (and still is) Sparky, sent a batch of his *Li'l Folks* panels to United Feature Syndicate. The editors there liked the panels and the roundheaded children who were featured in them. Nevertheless, the editors felt there were too many panels in newspapers at that time. They wanted to know if the cartoonist would be willing to draw his characters in the form of a comic strip, instead. Young Charles Schulz agreed, and the strip—renamed *Peanuts*—appeared in seven newspapers on October 2, 1950. Though he could not have known it then, Charles Schulz was on his way to fame and fortune. Today 200 million people in sixty-eight countries read the strip in languages familiar as Spanish where Charlie Brown is simply Carlitos. In a translation into Latin, however, good old Charlie Brown appears as Carolius Niger and Snoopy becomes Snupius.

Like all panels, *Li'l Folks* told a joke; *Peanuts*, along with all other comic strips, tells a story. The stories in comic strips are not like the kind of stories we read in books. A comic strip is really more like a play. The "stage" is the panels that make up the strip, and all of the "action" takes place in dialogue among the characters. And unlike a story in a book, a daily comic strip has few, if any, explanatory paragraphs.

Peanuts is translated into several foreign languages and read around the world.

If the funny incident is told in one series of panels, it is called a self-contained gag strip. *Beetle Bailey, Hagar the Horrible, Garfield, Calvin and Hobbes*, and *Mother Goose & Grimm* are all examples of this kind of self-contained gag strip. The story, or joke, ends on the same day that it begins in the newspaper. If the story continues over several days, the strip becomes a combination of gag and story strip.

Peanuts is an example of the kind of strip that usually is a self-contained gag strip, though at times it has a story line running through it. For example, Charles Schulz drew several strips about Linus's fears at night when he heard coyotes howling. The strips about the coyotes did not appear right after each other in *Peanuts*. Instead, that story was sprinkled throughout several weeks of the comic strip, mixed in with other gag strips about the different *Peanuts* characters.

Charles Schulz relaxes at home with his beloved dog, Andy.

Comic strips fall into two categories—the gag strip and the story (or narrative) strip. All of the funny comic strips are called gag strips, since *gag* is a slang word for "joke."

Mother Goose & Grimm
© TM 1993 Grimmy, Inc.
Licensed by MGM L&M.

There is really nothing funny about being afraid, and we do not laugh at Linus because he is afraid at night; we laugh because we know that howling coyotes cannot hurt him. We may also laugh because we recognize something about ourselves in those strips. Perhaps we, too, have been frightened at night, even though someone says, "There's nothing to be afraid of." And of course, we laugh at the way Linus tries to handle his fears and his friends' reactions to them.

Linus's fears were finally resolved, but that episode did not appear on a Saturday. In fact, if you follow *Peanuts*, you will never read the last installment of a story line on the last day of the week. Charles Schulz says, "You should never have anything end on Saturday. For some weird reason, people don't read the comics on Saturday, so I'll carry the story line over to Monday."

Occasionally, a gag strip will turn into a narrative strip if the cartoonist wants to build suspense. *Blondie* has been a mixture of gag and story strip for over sixty years, gathering new fans with each generation. In true comic strip fashion, *Blondie* has changed as life in the United States changes.

Blondie
© King Features Syndicate, Inc. Reprinted by special permission.

Blondie Boop-a-Doop was born in 1930, when America was in the Great Depression. People were out of work, and money was scarce. When cartoonist Chic Young first drew Blondie, she was a flapper, a term that was used in those days for young women who were beginning to find freedom from their traditional roles. Blondie had many boyfriends, including Dagwood Bumstead.

"Dagwood was the son of a billionaire," says Ted Hannah, director of advertising and public relations at King Features. "Dagwood fell in love with Blondie, but the family said, 'If you marry her, we will disown you.' " The comic strip ran for a while with the young couple dating despite Dagwood's family's disapproval. However, as Ted Hannah says, "*Blondie* as a comic strip was not very successful, and Chic Young was told by the comics editor of the syndicate to get them married. When they married and moved to Main Street, America, and started stories on the four universal themes—eating, sleeping, loving, and raising a family—the strip took off."

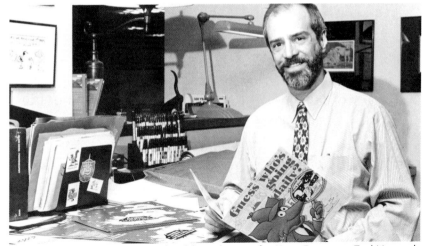

As director of Advertising and Public Relations for King Features, Ted Hannah keeps the public informed about the syndicate's comics.

After the wedding, Dagwood was disinherited. The newlyweds went on to establish a middle-class home. Like many other Americans, they had two children and a dog named Daisy who kept having puppies. Dagwood worked for a living and had a difficult boss, Mr. Dithers. Blondie stayed home and raised the children. Dagwood's famous sandwiches and naps on the sofa identified him to the public immediately. The Bumstead family was similar to many American families during that time. Readers could identify with them, and they loved to read about them.

Eventually, Chic Young died and his son, Dean, took over writing the strip. Stan Drake began drawing it. Dean Young continued his father's tradition of having the Bumsteads represent family life in the United States. However, life in America is different today than it was in 1930. In talking about *Blondie* during the 1990s, Dean Young says,

Chic Young's son, Dean, writes *Blondie* today.

Blondie
© King Features Syndicate, Inc. Reprinted by special permission.

16

"I work to keep the strip up-to-date." And how did he bring _Blondie_ into the '90s? He let his heroine get a job. Most American women work outside their homes today, and after sixty years as a homemaker, Blondie Bumstead went to work, too. For a while, Dean Young did not indicate in the strip exactly what kind of work Blondie would do. Americans were guessing about it and discussing it on television talk shows. The suspense built. It was as if the Bumsteads were everyone's relatives! Then, on Labor Day, 1991, the news came out—Blondie would work as a caterer. Anchor Peter Jennings reported Blondie's new job on ABC's nightly newscast, reading the strip out loud. He not only read the _Blondie_ strip on television but also named cartoonist Dean Young Person of the Week—a distinction that has included heads of state such as Mikhail Gorbachev.

Copyright © 1991 by WWT Partnership, Inc.

When Blondie went to work, she made the cover of national magazines.

Blondie
© King Features Syndicate, Inc. Reprinted by special permission.

Rex Morgan, M.D.
© North America Syndicate, Inc. Reprinted by special permission.

Although they have story lines that run through them, *Peanuts*, *Blondie*, and *Hi and Lois*, among others, are really gag strips. They rely on humor to bring the reader back to read them each day. In contrast, most story strips are not funny. Instead, they may have adventure in them, like *The Amazing Spider-Man*, or they may deal with a serious issue like the AIDS virus, as *Rex Morgan, M.D.* has done. *Prince Valiant* appears on Sunday and is another kind of narrative strip, based on the legend of King Arthur and his Knights of the Round Table. So gag strips can have a story in them, but most true story strips do not have jokes in them.

Like all artists everywhere, the cartoonists who create the comic strips we love have a vision of the world, a way of looking at things that they hope other people share. For example, Dean Young knows how hard it is to work for

Hagar the Horrible
© King Features Syndicate, Inc. Reprinted by special permission.

a difficult boss, so he puts Dagwood in that situation. Charles Schulz knows that people often wake up in the middle of the night, frightened, but they are not always sure what they are frightened of, and he draws strips about Linus being wakened by the coyotes' howling. Chris Browne realizes that even a Viking like Hagar might have a weight problem, and he puts that into his strip. All of these situations are familiar to most of us, and most of us think to ourselves when we read those strips, "Yes, that's how it is."

America's comics not only reflect "how it is" in our personal lives, they also show us "how it is" in our society. For years most professions, including cartooning, have been dominated by men. As a result of the women's movement and the civil rights movement, however, changes have been taking place in our society, and these changes are beginning to show up in the funny papers. Sarah Gillespie is the director of comic art for United Feature Syndicate, Inc., and she says, "Although in the past there have not been many comic strips by women cartoonists or cartoonists of color, more appear each year." *Jump Start* by Robb Armstrong and *Curtis* by Ray Billingsley are two examples of successful strips that feature African-American characters. And women like Cathy Guisewite and Lynn Johnston have created two very popular strips, *Cathy* and *For Better or Worse*, blazing a trail that other cartoonists are sure to follow.

Whether they are drawing panels or strips, telling jokes or stories, cartoonists are happiest when they think that someone has understood their message. Cartooning is hard work, but it is work that all cartoonists love and feel they simply must do. As Charles Schulz comments, "Why do musicians compose symphonies and poets write poems? They do it because life wouldn't have any meaning for them if they didn't. That's why I draw cartoons. It's my life."

Jump Start
reprinted by permission of UFS, Inc.

A Thomas Nast cartoon from *Harpers Weekly*, November 20, 1869

2

IN THEIR OPINION...

So far, we have talked about cartoons and comic strips, the jokes and stories the cartoonists want to tell, and the smiles their work brings to readers' faces. There is another kind of panel that is published in most daily papers, but this panel is not part of the comic pages. It is the editorial, or political, cartoon, and it appears in a section of the newspaper called the editorial pages. Traditionally, the editorial pages of a newspaper are the pages reserved for personal opinions, whether of columnists or readers.

People write letters to the editor to express their feelings about what is going on in their community or city, or even the country or the world. They write to the editor to explain what they like, or dislike, about their elected officials and to express their opinion about certain laws or behaviors. In short, a letter to the editor allows anyone to reach a large number of people and let them know how the letter-writer feels.

Human beings have opinions about a variety of subjects, but many people do not realize that newspapers have opinions, too. After all, newspapers report the news, and the reporters' personal opinions are not supposed to find their way into their stories. A news story should deal with facts, and facts only.

However, a newspaper as a whole usually does have a political philosophy. Like people, the newspaper may have a liberal philosophy—believing in social reform in politics and being open to new ideas. Or a paper may be conservative in its viewpoint—believing in caution and keeping things as they are. The political philosophy of any newspaper is usually similar to that of its publisher and the editor in chief, and the editorial page of the paper is the place where that opinion is expressed. Sometimes newspapers will take a stand on an issue or endorse a political candidate whom they feel best represents the paper's political philosophy by writing articles called *editorials*. There is one other way editorial opinion is expressed in the newspaper; it is much shorter than an editorial, and much funnier. It is the editorial cartoon.

An editorial cartoon expresses the political opinions of the cartoonist—and for the most part, of the newspaper that runs the cartoon. Though they can be funny, most editorial cartoons have a serious side. They are meant to persuade people to take a certain point of view. Almost

© North America Syndicate, Inc. Reprinted by special permission.

every daily paper in America prints at least one editorial cartoon. If the paper is in a big city and has a large circulation—a lot of people who purchase it—there may be a person on the paper's staff who is the editorial cartoonist. Some editorial cartoonists are as popular as the comic strip cartoonists, and their political cartoons may appear in newspapers across the country. In fact, some favorite comic strip cartoonists began their careers drawing editorial cartoons. Some, like Mike Peters, draw both.

Mike Peters was an editorial cartoonist before he ever created *Mother Goose & Grimm*. He got his first profes-

Prize, the most prestigious journalism award, in 1981, for his editorial cartooning. In 1984, he created *Mother Goose & Grimm*, but he still produces four editorial cartoons every week, cartoons that are circulated to newspapers across the country.

Thomas Nast was one of the United States's most influential editorial cartoonists. He lived during the time of the Civil War and published his cartoons in *Harper's Weekly*. In an age before telephones, radio, or television, people got much of their information from newspapers,

Mike Peters draws editorial cartoons in addition to *Mother Goose & Grimm*.

WELL,, THEY SAID THEY WERE ONLY HIRING QUALIFIED GREYHOUND DRIVERS...

Reprinted by permission of Tribune Media Services.

sional job when he was only thirteen years old, drawing editorial cartoons for the *Webster Kirkwood Advertiser* in St. Louis, Missouri. "I did cartoons about the mayor, the local water rates, potholes in the streets," he says. From that beginning, Mike Peters went on to win a Pulitzer

"Stranger Things Have Happened. Hold On, and You May Walk Over the Sluggish Animal Up There Yet," a Thomas Nast cartoon from _Harpers Weekly_, December 27, 1879

and Nast's cartoons were widely read. During the Civil War, he drew several editorial cartoons that supported the position of the North. President Abraham Lincoln appreciated Nast's cartoons and called him "our best recruiting sergeant." In countries that have free speech and a free press, the editorial cartoon is a time-honored tradition. No one should be surprised to read that the United States uses the editorial cartoon more than any other country in the world.

An editorial cartoon rarely says anything nice about a person or an institution. Editorial cartoonists are usually upset about something or someone when they draw their cartoons. The cartoon is a way of calling attention to something in our society that the cartoonist thinks is wrong. The cartoonist usually makes fun of the current state of affairs by using a kind of humor called satire. One day, various cartoonists may ridicule corporate greed, on another day they will make fun of racism, and another day they may mock the Congress of the United States. No one is safe from their pens—not even the president of the country! However, the main purpose of these cartoons is to make people think, not to hurt anyone's feelings.

Satire, making fun of something by appearing to treat it seriously, can be a very powerful weapon when it is turned on a situation that is wrong. Editorial cartoonist Jimmy Margulies has used satire to call attention to parents' and students' concern about the violence in many American schools.

Cartoonists have always relied on visual symbols to help

24

By using that symbol, it is very clear that his editoria cartoon is ridiculing cigarette smoking and the effect it has on a person's body and appearance.

Sometimes a cartoonist will create a symbol that endures. Thomas Nast developed the symbols of the donkey for the Democratic party and the elephant for the Republican party, and these are still used and instantly recognized today. When people see the figure of Uncle Sam, they know that he represents the United States government—there is no need for the cartoonist to explain that fact. In a cartoon, you may see Uncle Sam warning a foreign government or welcoming a dignitary. In the cartoon

them get their message across. In an editorial cartoon, the symbols become very important. Although they are fine for the gag cartoonist, light bulbs for ideas and stars for pain are simply not enough for the editorial cartoon. If an editorial cartoonist has any doubt that people will understand the symbolism in his cartoon, he will label the item clearly. In Margulies's cartoon, we know the man is a school principal, because his desk has a label on it.

Editorial cartoonists rely on other kinds of symbols to get their message across, too. Instead of talking about cigarettes, cartoonist Steve Benson has used Joe Cool, the camel that has long been the symbol for Camel cigarettes.

© King Features Syndicate, Inc. Reprinted by special permission.

Drawing caricatures can be fun, but it is also work, like any other form of cartooning.

Naturally, someone who draws an editorial cartoon must be a good reader. He or she has to be aware of many things that are happening in our society, in order to be ready to joke about them in a cartoon. And the cartoonist needs to have a strong opinion about what is going on. Editorial cartooning is not a business for people who, like Charlie Brown, are wishy-washy. But it certainly is a business for someone who has a sense of humor.

above, you see another symbol for the United States, the Statue of Liberty. But this time, she is not welcoming anyone, not even the Haitian refugees. What message is this cartoonist trying to communicate?

If a cartoonist is drawing a famous person, such as the president of the United States or a celebrity from the entertainment world, he draws that person in caricature. A caricature is a picture of something or someone that exaggerates any feature—such as Bill Clinton's nose—that is distinctive about the subject. It is that feature that the cartoonist will distort, just to make his picture funny.

"Bill Clinton" © 1993 by
David Small

26

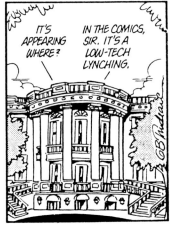

We have said that all writers, including those who write comic strips and comic books, have a vision of the world that they want to communicate to their readers. However, most cartoonists avoid putting their political opinions in their daily comic strips. Mike Peters says that because he draws four editorial cartoons a week, he does not feel that he has to put his political opinions in *Mother Goose & Grimm.* Not all cartoonists share his views, of course, and sometimes editorial opinion creeps into the comic strips.

Garry Trudeau's *Doonesbury* is a very popular comic strip that often expresses Mr. Trudeau's opinions. By using satire, the kind of humor all political cartoonists love, Garry Trudeau's *Doonesbury* has poked fun at the leaders of the United States, crime figures, and entertainers, among others. In 1975, Garry Trudeau won a Pulitzer Prize for his comic strips that dealt with the Watergate stories and scandal during President Richard Nixon's term in office. Mr. Trudeau will not allow *Doonesbury* to be shrunk to fit the standard comic pages of a newspaper. Because the strip is larger and may at times reflect Mr. Trudeau's personal political opinions, *Doonesbury* is often run on the editorial pages of newspapers. As you can tell from the strip on this page, in Mr. Trudeau's opinion at least, even the people in the White House pay attention to the comics!

Since the founding of our country, the rights to free speech and a free press have been practiced and protected. We are free to say what we want, when we want to say it; and—if someone will publish it—we can share our views with readers around the world. As long as our Constitution protects free speech and the freedom of the press, there will be editorial cartoons and editorial comic strips in America's newspapers.

Hank Ketcham

A BRIGHT IDEA

All creative work is both an event and a process. The event is the moment when the idea first comes to the artist, inventor, writer, composer, scientist—whoever is doing the creating. Of course, an idea is nothing until it is put to some use, and that is the part of creativity that is a process—putting an idea to work. Like any other art form, the art of creating comics has to have both these elements, the idea and then the execution of it. However, ideas are a bit like humor. No one knows exactly how to make an idea—or a laugh—happen. Nevertheless, inspiration occasionally comes from simple things right at home.

   In 1950, Hank Ketcham's son, Dennis, was a mischievous four-year-old. One afternoon the little boy had been particularly Dennis-like and had totally messed up his bedroom. When she saw the wreckage, Dennis's mother exclaimed to his father, "Your son is a menace!" Hmm . . . Hank Ketcham thought. Dennis the Menace. He immediately began to draw a few panels based on the actions of a lively little boy who got into trouble without meaning to, and a classic cartoon character was born.

Hank Ketcham and many other cartoonists often find that trouble is the inspiration for the ideas and characters in their cartoons and comic strips. Mike Peters's bull terrier, Grimm, is frequently in trouble, and some of Grimm's problems in the strip may be inspired by Mike Peters's own problems as a child. Although he began cartooning when he was five years old and drew pictures to illustrate the stories his mother told him, Mike Peters had a hard time in school.

"I was a terrible student," he says today. "In fact, I deliberately did not go to school on the last day of third grade because I was sure I had failed. I just showed up for fourth grade in the fall, then waited for them to come get me, if they were going to move me back. Cartooning was one thing I did well."

Mike Peters finished fourth grade and all the other grades, then went on to college. All the time, he kept on cartooning and struggling with school. Later, when this Pulitzer Prize winner was talking to Eric Siegel of *The Baltimore Sun* about *Mother Goose & Grimm*, he said, "A cartoonist has to tap into himself or herself and put that person into the strip. The strip has to reflect what the cartoonist believes. You can't write a strip just to tell gags. The artist truly has to be in the main character. When I realized that I *was* Grimm, my strip took off."

That method of creativity must work, because a young fan named Matt Jones talks about *Mother Goose & Grimm* and says, "I like it because Grimm is always getting into trouble and doing weird stuff to make me laugh." Mike Peters's struggles with school are over, but they now give him ideas for his strip.

Copr. 1951, Post-Hall Syndicate, Inc.

13

"GO AHEAD DADDY — SQUIRT IT RIGHT IN HIS EYE!"

Dennis the Menace
© North America Syndicate, Inc. Reprinted by special permission.

Mother Goose & Grimm
© TM 1993 Grimmy, Inc. Licensed by MGM L&M.

Sometimes an idea comes from something deep inside the cartoonist, like Mike Peters saying he *is* Grimm, and sometimes it comes from inspiration outside of the cartoonist, like the comment Dennis Ketcham's mother made. However, there are times when an idea comes only after a lot of hard work, concentration, and a desire to create something different. Dik Browne, who collaborated with Mort Walker on *Hi and Lois* until his death in 1989, created his own strip, *Hagar the Horrible*, using deliberate hard work. His son, Chris, continues to write and draw that strip today. In talking about the beginnings of *Hagar the Horrible*, Chris says, "My father wanted a strip of his own, with his own characters. One day he told my mother he was going down to our basement and wasn't coming

Hagar the Horrible
© King Features Syndicate, Inc. Reprinted by special permission.

Beetle Bailey
© King Features Syndicate,
Inc. Reprinted by special
permission.

up until he had created a new character and strip. We didn't know how long that might take!" Dik Browne took food and blankets down to that basement with him. Fortunately for the Brownes, Dik emerged after only six hours with five complete strips of that famous Viking, Hagar the Horrible.

So a comic strip or panel begins with an idea and one or more characters who will help the cartoonist get his or her idea across to the reader. And how does a cartoonist create these kinds of characters? That isn't easy, either! Mort Walker has created dozens of lovable comic people, including Hi and Lois and Beetle Bailey, and yet he says, "One of the hardest parts of being a cartoonist is breathing life into the characters." When Beetle Bailey first appeared in the comic pages on September 4, 1950, he was not a work-shirking private in the army—he was a work-shirking student in college, and the United States was

fighting in Korea. In true comic strip fashion, Mort Walker had his college student join the army, where Beetle has remained—still a private—for more than forty years. Originally, the strip was carried in twelve newspapers. As a college student, Beetle was not particularly popular with readers, but when he joined the army, his popularity soared. Today his adventures appear in 1,800 newspapers scattered around the world. Even Mort Walker is not sure why Beetle succeeded more as an army private than he did as a college student. Perhaps Beetle's new popularity had something to do with the fact that there were tens of thousands of World War II veterans at the time and far fewer college students. Perhaps not. There are some parts of creativity that will always be a mystery.

Sometimes one comic strip will provide inspiration for another, different strip. In 1954, Beetle Bailey got a leave and went home to visit his family. Civilian life did not

Beetle Bailey
© King Features Syndicate, Inc. Reprinted by special permission.

agree with Beetle, and he returned to Camp Swampy, but two members of his family, Hi and Lois, turned up later in a strip of their own about family life in America.

Dik Browne and Mort Walker's collaboration on *Hi and Lois* has become a family tradition. Today another of Dik Browne's sons, Chance, draws that strip, and it is written by Mort Walker's sons, Brian and Greg. Because he grew up as the son of a cartoonist, Brian Walker knows a lot about creating comic strips and the characters that inhabit them. Talking about his brother and himself, Brian Walker says, "We *were* the characters in *Hi and Lois* when we were little. Now we have to look for ideas in our own families, but our kids are growing up. Fortunately, Chance still has little ones! It isn't easy work. I'm not a gag machine, and no comic strip is funny every single day."

That is true for all comic strips—none of them is funny every single day, and that is why the characters in the strips are so important. In the cartoonist's world, those characters do not have to be human—they can be cats, dogs, even stuffed tigers—but no matter what kind of

Brian Walker, Chance Browne, and Greg Walker *(left to right)* try out their latest gags during their weekly meeting.

33

Hagar the Horrible

creatures they are, they must have human characteristics. In other words, they must have real personalities. They must feel, think, and communicate, so that readers feel they know them and, knowing them, can care about them. In order for a comic strip to become a success and last through the years, people must remain interested in the characters, be willing to read the strip on the days when it isn't very funny, and look forward to those days when the characters' behavior makes them laugh out loud.

In his play *Romeo and Juliet*, William Shakespeare has Juliet ask, "What's in a name?" A cartoonist would probably answer, "Everything!" Bill Rechin and Don Wilder work together to bring us *Crock,* a strip about foreign legionnaires stuck in the desert. Don writes the strip, and he says, "I can't come up with a full character until I get the name. Names are more important in comic strips than anywhere else. A name should be short, so the reader can

Bill Rechin and Don Wilder pose in their studio with Quench, the camel.

Crock
© North America Syndicate, Inc. Reprinted by special permission.

remember it." It is true that names tell us something about the character. With a name like Vermin P. Crock, can you imagine what the character will be like?

Charlie Brown, Frieda, and Linus were all named after friends of Charles Schulz's during the days before *Peanuts,* when he taught at the Art Instruction Schools, Inc. "I was the one who called Charles Brown 'Charlie,'" Charles Schulz says. "I used to introduce him at parties by saying something like, 'Here comes good old Charlie Brown. Now we're going to have a good time.'" The phrase "Good ol' Charlie Brown" appeared in the first *Peanuts* strip and, along with sayings like "Happiness is a warm puppy," is part of our language today.

But a handful of cleverly named characters is not enough to bring a comic strip to life. The next problem is story ideas. As Brian Walker says, "There's never a paid vacation in cartooning. You have to fill that space in the paper every day, 365 days a year, whether you're sick or not." Writing a comic strip is a little like being in show business—rain or shine, the show must go on.

But where do the ideas for those strips come from? And how is it possible to think of fresh new ideas day after day, week in and week out, for years and years? A cartoonist is always on the lookout for these moments in life that can be turned into a good panel or strip. Dik Browne disappeared into his basement to create *Hagar the Horrible.* No one can say exactly what took place as Hagar was being born, but Chris Browne says his father always kept a notebook with him, jotting down bits and pieces of ideas as they came to him. Surely that notebook went down into the basement with Dik Browne, and perhaps somewhere in those pages was the idea for the lovable Viking who lives on today.

In fact, many cartoonists keep a notepad handy so that

Hagar the Horrible
© King Features Syndicate, Inc. Reprinted by special permission.

they can record the funny things happening to them—or to someone else—during the day. Later, those observations might suggest a caption for a cartoon. Hank Ketcham advises all young people who might want to have a career in cartooning to keep this kind of notebook. "You can put anything in it, but boil it down," he says. "Just note, 'Dad got mad at the dog' or something. But make it funny. And be sure to look at it every night."

Mr. Ketcham's advice is good, and it works for him. However, there are as many ways of writing and drawing a comic strip as there are strips to read, and no two cartoonists work exactly the same way.

Though he draws all of the art himself and keeps a notebook of ideas, Hank Ketcham also buys ideas from gag writers. "I have a team of them who submit ideas to me. I've become a good editor through the years. I know what will work for Dennis, so I buy what I like and reject the rest. Buying material from other writers helps the humor

"YOU GOTTA EXPECT SEASONAL SLUMPS, JOEY."

Dennis the Menance
© North America Syndicate, Inc. Reprinted by special permission.

Peanuts
reprinted by permission of
UFS, Inc.

in Dennis stay fresh," Mr. Ketcham says.

The gag writers submit a suggestion for the picture and the words that make the picture funny. For example, they might say, "Dennis is trying to sell lemonade outside in the middle of the winter and says, 'You gotta expect seasonal slumps, Joey.'" Mr. Ketcham's art, with its attention to detail, is why these gags work so successfully. The picture *looks* cold, and the lemonade does not look appealing. That is what makes the caption work. Hank Ketcham says, "I always want the art to be exquisite," and it is.

Hank Ketcham is one of many cartoonists who buy gags. On the other hand, Charles Schulz writes every word and draws every line that go into *Peanuts*. "In forty-two years I've never used anybody else's ideas," he says. When asked if it is difficult to come up with new ideas after so many years of work, he replies simply, "It's what I do. The cur-

tain goes up, you walk on stage, and do it."

Different things will suggest ideas for *Peanuts*. Charles Schulz likes to draw Peppermint Patty and Marcie at the concert hall. When he came upon a piece of music by composer Benjamin Britten called *A Young Person's Guide to the Orchestra*, he thought there might be an idea there, but it didn't come to him right away. Instead, he jotted the title on a piece of paper and put it on his desk where he could see it each day. He thought about it for a month, and then his idea came to him. "I'm finally going to draw it next week," he said. "I've decided that Patty and Marcie will be at the concert hall. Marcie will hold a program that has 'A Young Person's Guide to the Orchestra by Benjamin Britten' on it. Patty'll turn to Marcie and ask, 'Why do we need a guide to the orchestra if they're sitting right in front of us?'" And so, another *Peanuts* strip is born, this one inspired by a famous piece of music.

Don Wilder is one of the fortunate cartoonists who seem to have an endless supply of ideas. "I read a lot as a child and I read now," he says. "I get ideas everywhere: from books, the movies, from people I meet (especially Bill Rechin's friends—they're pretty funny), maybe just a funny word I hear. I'm like a sponge, and I soak everything up. There's a lot of sad humor in Crock's situation, being stuck in the desert with the heat, and flies, and lack of food." Once again, we see that cartoonists often use a potentially sad or frightening situation to create humor. After Don Wilder comes up with the idea, he writes the strip and hands it to his partner, friend, and neighbor Bill Rechin, who says, "After I read it, I can't wait to draw it."

Of course, it is cartoon art that makes a panel or strip a comic. But the words are as important as the art. As Mort Walker says, "Half of the work is in the writing. You have to educate yourself, take writing courses. Everything you are comes out in your work. If you're dumb, everyone knows it." And his son Greg adds, "Comics are a bit like poetry. The writer is distilling something down to its basic elements. There is an art to whittling something down. If you want to be a cartoonist, you have to learn how to write."

All authors choose their words carefully; however, book authors have the luxury of using hundreds, perhaps thousands, of words to get their story told. In a comic strip, there is no room for even one extra word, so each must be chosen carefully. Every word is a working word.

Although each cartoonist gets ideas and then executes them in his or her own way, there are certain rules that apply to every successful comic strip. If you read the comic pages carefully, you will see that all cartoonists follow these rules. One rule is consistency. Although they will change slightly throughout the years, in general comic characters have to look the same, panel after panel, week after week—and they must act the same, too. Part of the

Crock
© North America Syndicate, Inc. Reprinted by special permission.

Beetle Bailey
© King Features Syndicate, Inc. Reprinted by special permission.

humor in a strip lies in your knowing exactly what the characters will do in a given situation. Charlie Brown will always love the little red-haired girl, and the readers will never see her. And when asked if poor old Charlie Brown will ever kick the football, Charles Schulz answers quickly, "No. You can't ruin things." It is true that people do not expect Charlie Brown to kick the ball, and they might be disappointed if he did. Talking about Charlie and the football, Charles Schulz says, "The reader can read into the strip whatever he or she thinks. Either Char-

lie Brown's awfully stupid, or he's naive, or Lucy's awfully mean." Charles Schulz pauses for a moment, then smiles and adds, "Or else Charlie Brown's one of these people who have a lot of faith in human nature."

When readers start thinking about a character, wondering why the character behaves as he or she does, and look forward to reading the strip or panel every day, the cartoonist knows that the idea has worked. The characters have come to life and live on in the imaginations of their creator and the readers.

Peanuts
reprinted by permission of UFS, Inc.

Charles Schulz

FUNNY PICTURES

"I draw funny pictures. That's what I do," says Charles Schulz, explaining his occupation. "Drawing is so important. You must be able to draw the characters so they're fun to look at." On the subject of drawing funny pictures, Hank Ketcham comments, "If I had to choose between the caption and the picture, I'd want the picture to be funny regardless of what was said."

Being fun to look at is one thing that sets cartoon art apart from all other kinds of art. No matter how carefully cartoon characters are conceived, named, and written about, they could not exist without the distinctive pictures that help tell their stories.

Although cartoon people are not realistic, they must *seem* real. A child must look like a child, an adult like a parent, a teacher, a burglar, or a doctor—there can be no mistaking who they are. The cartoonist has no space to waste on explanations, so he or she will often rely on exaggeration and visual symbols to explain characters. In fact, many times it is the exaggeration that makes the joke.

Cartoonists work very hard to perfect their drawing skills. Chris Browne remembers his father, Dik, helping him learn to be a cartoon artist. "When I was ten years old, my father sat me down with a sketchbook and told me to draw circles. That's all—just circles. It sounds simple, but it was hard to do. My circles were wobbly. When I had filled pages with circles and felt I had them down, I took my book to my father. He looked at it and simply said, 'Now ovals.' " Chris Browne points out that practically all cartoon art consists of curving lines, and the practice he had long ago has made him able to control his pencil. "The pencil goes where *I* want it to go," he

says. "And I still draw circles for practice." The early lessons provided inspiration for a *Hagar the Horrible* strip.

Cartoon art has a unique style that sets it apart from other kinds of art, and cartoon artists have styles of their own, too. If Hank Ketcham, Charles Schulz, and Mike Peters drew sketches of the same scene but did not sign them or put Dennis, Snoopy, or Grimmy in the picture, you would probably be able to tell which artist drew each picture. Why? Because you recognize each artist's style—a way of drawing that is theirs, and theirs alone. Just as Picasso's work does not look like Rembrandt's, and Rembrandt's does not look like Van Gogh's, *Blondie* does not look or sound like *Peanuts*, and *Peanuts* does not look or sound like *Prince Valiant*.

In general, if a strip is funny, the drawing will *look* funny. If it is a more serious strip, like *Rex Morgan, M.D.*, it may be drawn very realistically. And if it is an adventure

Hagar the Horrible
© King Features Syndicate, Inc. Reprinted by special permission.

The Amazing Spider-Man
© 1993 Marvel Entertainment Group, Inc. All rights reserved.

of a superhero, like *The Amazing Spider-Man*, the art may be semi-realistic. Of course, through the years the characters (and their artists) may change. Today's *Blondie* is written by Dean Young and drawn by Stan Drake. Blondie may not look exactly like the flapper who appeared more than sixty years ago, but everyone knows it is the same lady. Even if the same cartoonist continues to draw the strip, the characters may change. Snoopy began his comic life walking on four feet like a normal dog. Today he walks upright, but he still looks like Snoopy. Nevertheless, once a strip's style is established, it remains the same throughout the years. Anyone who helps the cartoonist with penciling or lettering or inking must be able to copy the strip's style perfectly.

Blondie
© King Features Syndicate, Inc. Reprinted by special permission.

Some strips, however, end when their creator retires or dies. Al Capp's *Li'l Abner* stopped when the cartoonist died, and Charles Schulz has said that *Peanuts* will stop when he retires. "No one continued to draw Picasso's pictures after he died," Mr. Schulz says. Although he has continued to draw the strip his father created, Chris Browne understands when an artist doesn't want his or her strip to be drawn by someone else—even if the "someone" was the cartoonist's child. "A comic strip is a real expression of the cartoonist's soul and outlook," he says. "It's such a personal thing." Then he adds, "I have my own vision of Hagar now."

In the early days of *Beetle Bailey* and, later, *Hi and Lois*, Mort Walker, along with Chris Browne's father, Dik, developed a unique way of producing daily episodes of their strips. More than one person worked on those strips then, yet the strips have maintained their style. Now that their sons have inherited *Hi and Lois* and *Hagar the Horrible*, they follow the same practice.

"Brian and I work separately on ideas," says Greg Walker. "We get together every two weeks, usually on Mondays, for a gag conference. Sometimes we meet with our dad and do *Beetle* and *Hi and Lois* gags at the same time." Whether they are meeting with Mort Walker or by themselves, each member of the team brings between fifteen and thirty gags to the conference. The gags are not

Hi and Lois © King Features Syndicate, Inc. Reprinted by special permission.

Beetle Bailey © King Features Syndicate, Inc. Reprinted by special permission.

just typewritten lists of jokes. Comic art is a careful combination of picture and words, so each gag includes a rough sketch of the strip, complete with the words in their balloons.

"It's important that the gags be drawn, as well as written," explains Brian Walker. "The person who is talking, where they are, how the person feels—all those things can influence whether the gag is funny or not." Chance Browne, who draws *Hi and Lois*, agrees that the art is an important part of the gag.

The three men divide the gags among themselves and grade them. A mark of I means definitely use it. II means the gag needs some work, and III means it needs to be put aside for even more work. "We also use pluses and minuses," Greg Walker says. "I+ means this is the greatest gag you've ever written in your whole life and we have to use it immediately!" He is smiling when he says that.

When the ideas are in place and the rough sketches are finished, the cartoonist is ready to create the finished art.

Comic strips look as if they are sketched quickly, almost casually, but that is far from the truth. A comic strip is a carefully designed piece of art. The cartoonist must decide on two important elements in his or her art—composition and perspective. Composition deals with how the picture will be arranged. What should be shown? How much background is necessary? What should be left out? These are some of the questions artists ask as they compose their pictures.

Cartoonists also think about perspective, the way things look from a given point. Should the perspective be up close and tight, focusing only on the characters' faces? That will add drama to the strip. You often see a close perspective in a story strip like *Rex Morgan, M.D.*, because the artist wants to show the drama of the moment. Dr. Christine Slater is an emergency room physician who appeared in *Rex Morgan, M.D.* In the strip's story line, Dr. Slater accidentally became infected with the AIDS virus while caring for a patient. In the episodes that deal with Dr. Slater's sharing the news that she is HIV positive, Tony DiPreta, who draws the strip, often focused tightly on the doctor's

face, to show how concerned she is about the effect this news will have on her family.

Sometimes the cartoonist will use perspective to help him get the gag across to the reader. One panel could be drawn in which we see the characters up close, and in the next we could see the scene larger and from a distance. It is that bigger picture that helps get the joke across. In *Hi and Lois*, the cartoonists decided to poke a little fun at people's interest in having four-wheel-drive cars— whether they need one or not. Chance Browne drew the first panel close up, then moved back for a broader perspective that showed a flat driveway, suitable for any kind of car. It is the picture, not the words, that makes the joke in that strip.

Rex Morgan, M.D.

Hi and Lois © King Features Syndicate, Inc. Reprinted by special permission.

At other times, a strip will be drawn with a single perspective, one that is not up close or too far away. *Blondie* is usually drawn that way. So are *Peanuts*, *Beetle Bailey*, and many others. The characters in the strip, the background, and the perspective all combine to make up the composition of the art. Once the cartoonist has decided on the strip's composition, he or she is ready to create the finished product.

Bridge

FINISHING TOUCHES

From the first hint that an idea is coming to the last stroke of the pen, every successful cartoonist is a working cartoonist. Charles Schulz works in his studio five days a week. So do Hank Ketcham, all of the Walkers, the Brownes, Mike Peters, Bill Rechin, and Don Wilder. In fact, all of the other cartoonists who are publishing their strips know they must practice self-discipline and get to their drawing boards every single day of the work week. Paraphrasing Thomas Edison, who was talking about genius, Brian Walker says getting ideas involves 99 percent perspiration and 1 percent inspiration. "I think everyone is creative," he says. "But you have to go to work." Brother Greg adds, "You can be the most fantastic talent in the world, but if you don't get your work done, you don't have a job." And Mike Peters adds three words to this advice: "Practice, practice, practice."

However, all the hard work and practice will not remove the cartoonists' biggest problem today—space. Although every daily paper in the United States, with the exception of the *New York Times,* the *Wall Street Journal,* the *Chris-tian Science Monitor,* and *USA Today,* has a comic section, humor is still not as important to newspaper editors as other kinds of material. The sad truth is, the comics are being squeezed into less and less space on newspaper pages, and the art of the cartoonist suffers for it.

Hank Ketcham is glad to be drawing a panel during the week, saving his strip for Sundays only. "One nice thing about the panel that I do on weekdays is the space I have to work in," he says. "All of the space in that panel is mine. I have room for the graphics [the picture] because the caption goes below it."

The original strip or panel that the artist draws is always much bigger than the comic that appears in your daily paper. Unfortunately, by the time people read the comics, much of the detail in the original drawings is lost because the strip has been photographically reduced, then printed on an inexpensive paper called newsprint. Although it is fine for our daily papers, which are recycled or thrown away, newsprint is not good paper on which to reproduce art.

In talking about comic strip art, Charles Schulz says, "There's something fascinating about seeing the originals. They're so much better than what we see in the newspaper." Mr. Schulz is right. Most people are very surprised when they see an original comic strip, just as the artist drew it. The details that are missed in the paper jump out at them, and they realize that they are looking at real art, not sketches.

Although each cartoonist has his or her own way of

"THAT'S WHERE I KEEP MY COLLECTION OF THINGS I FIND UNDER ROCKS."

A special camera copies the original comic strip and reduces its size.

drawing and inking, comic strips are generally drawn in stages, and more than one person may be involved. Usually, the dialogue goes in first; then it is surrounded by something unique to the comics—a balloon with a tail or bubbles. Some cartoonists will just draw the balloon and leave it blank for another person, called a letterer, to put in the words later. But Chance Browne doesn't believe in doing his art for *Hi and Lois* that way. "The lettering has to be a certain size to be readable," he says. "I don't like to look at the balloon and think, 'Maybe it'll be big enough,' so I letter in every word myself." Later, the letterer will ink in the words.

Of course, some comic strips do not use balloons at all, because they would interfere with the strip's style. *Prince Valiant* first appeared in 1937. It was written and drawn by Hal Foster, and if you look carefully at its title in a Sunday paper it now says *Hal Foster's Prince Valiant* by John Cullen Murphy. Mr. Murphy was Hal Foster's assistant; when Mr. Foster retired in 1970, John Cullen Murphy began to draw the strip. However, like many other strips, *Prince Valiant* has turned into a family affair. Mr. Murphy says, "I'm an illustrator, not a cartoonist. I've got to have something to draw." The "something" that John Cullen Murphy draws is the weekly episode that is carefully researched and written by his son, Cullen Murphy. The legend of King Arthur has been around for centuries, and each week Cullen Murphy adds a bit to it. "It helps that Cullen has a degree in medieval European history from Amherst College," says his father.

John Cullen Murphy illustrates *Prince Valiant* in a realistic style.

AND THEY ARE MET. AND, AS ONE, THE THRONG IN THE STANDS TURNS AWAY IN DISBELIEF, AND THEN CRINGES IN HORROR. THE DEFEAT OF PRINCE VALIANT AND HIS MEN IS TOTAL AND IGNOMINIOUS. FOUR "OLD MEN," AS ALL BELIEVE THEM TO BE, HAVE UNSEATED THE PRIDE OF BRITISH CHIVALRY.

IN THE SILENCE THAT FOLLOWS, GUNDERIT'S MEN DISMOUNT. KING ARTHUR BESTOWS THE PURSE UPON THEM....A SMALL FORTUNE. BUT NEVER DO THEY REMOVE THEIR HELMETS, FOR DOING SO WOULD EXPOSE GUNDERIT'S DECEIT. THESE VETERANS OF THE SIRMIUM WAR THAT THEODORIC WAGED AGAINST THE GEPIDS SIMPLY ACCEPT THE MONEY, TURN, AND LEAD THEIR MOUNTS AWAY. IT IS THEN THAT ALETA NOTICES SOMETHING PECULIAR.

NEXT WEEK: Too Spry.

© 1989 King Features Syndicate, Inc. World rights reserved

11-5   2752

JOHN CULLEN MURPHY

Prince Valiant © King Features Syndicate, Inc. Reprinted by special permission.

When John Cullen Murphy is finished with his illustration of his son's story, he sends the package to Florida, where his daughter, Mairead "Meg" Nash, lives. Meg's job is to color the Sunday-only strip and letter in the story without using balloons because, as her father says, "I worry about the picture's composition—putting it together in the right way."

In addition to balloons, there are certain other symbols that originated with the comics. Mort Walker has written an entire book, *The Lexicon of Comicana*, which takes a lighthearted look at the symbols that he called *symbolia*. Most readers recognize *symbolia* the minute they see them. A light bulb over a character's head always means a bright idea is coming; stars usually mean something hurts. And a group of stars, exclamation points, and asterisks clustered together means the character is using

Hagar the Horrible
© King Features Syndicate, Inc. Reprinted by special permission.

words that are not fit to print, as Hagar is doing in the strip on this page. Beads of perspiration show that a character is either worried or working hard. Exclamation points by themselves show astonishment or surprise.

Besides these visual symbols, the comics have added certain words and expressions to our language as well. Charlie Brown's resigned "Good grief!" or frustrated "Rats!" in *Peanuts* are two examples of expressions that

originated in the funny papers and found their way into our daily conversations. Also, words like *whap* and *plop* have come into our vocabularies (and dictionaries) because they provided sound effects for the funny papers. In *Nancy*, Jerry Scott has used a combination of sound effects and symbolia to emphasize Nancy's fate. A star, exclamation point, bold "crunch" and drawn-out "o-o-o-o-n" leave little doubt about her fall from the tree.

Nancy
reprinted by permission of UFS, Inc.

Once the balloons, the background, the characters, and any symbols are penciled in, the strip is ready to be inked. Some cartoonists do their own inking, as well as penciling, and others leave the inking to artists who are called—well—inkers. Finally, the borders go around each panel, and the strip is finished—if it is a daily. Creating the Sunday funnies is a more involved procedure.

The Sunday funnies, in color, have been around for nearly one hundred years. William Randolph Hearst, who owned the *New York Journal*, created the first Sunday comic section for the paper. When it appeared in the *Journal* in 1896, the section was advertised as "eight pages of polychromatic effulgence that make the rainbow look like a lead pipe." *Polychromatic* refers to something that has many colors, and *effulgence* means something that shines brilliantly—one wonders how many readers of the old *Journal* understood what the paper was talking about! Of course, the Sunday funnies were wildly popular, and soon papers all around the country were copying Hearst and adding their own colored comic sections.

In the early years of the comics, the cartoonists colored their Sunday strips themselves. Many still do, because they want to see what the finished product will look like. Some, like John Cullen Murphy, leave the coloring to others.

Cartoonists may choose their colors from among 123 different shades of red, orange, yellow, blue, green, and violet. Each color is given a number and is printed on a chart supplied by the printer of most of America's comics,

Using the color chart as a guide, John Cullen Murphy codes a Sunday strip for color.

American Color in Buffalo, New York. For example, the lightest shade of pink may be number 2, a slightly darker shade is 3, and an even deeper shade of the same color is 4. Yellow comes in shades 5, 9, 13, and 68. If a cartoonist colors the strip, he still must put the numbers of the colors on each piece of clothing, blade of grass, stick of furniture. Every single thing in the strip gets a color number, except something that will be white or black. All the strips are outlined and inked in black, and if white is needed, the cartoonist lets the plain white paper show through. When the Sunday comic is colored, or color-coded, it is ready to be sent to the syndicate.

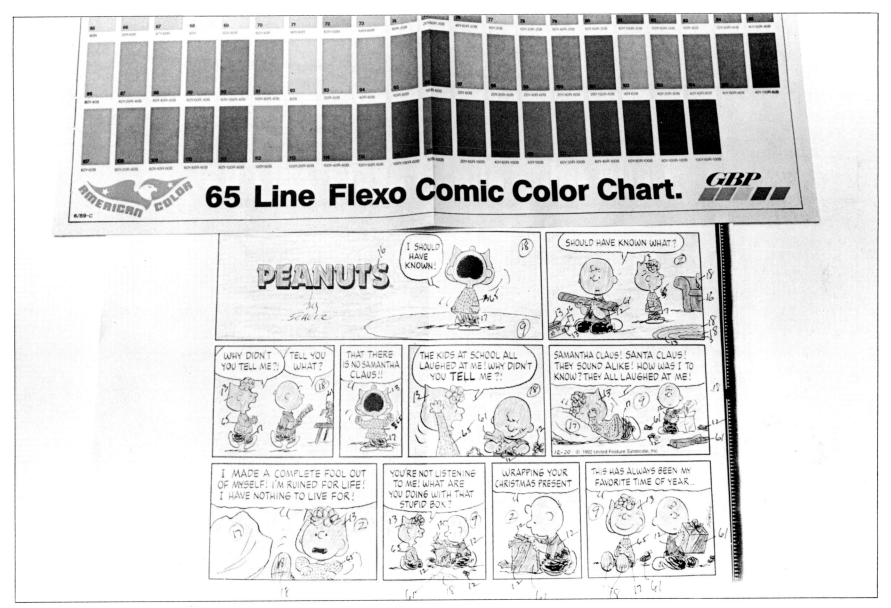

The numbers on *Peanuts* correspond to the numbers on the chart.

Paul Hendricks of King Features Syndicate

GETTING SYNDICATED

You have already read about the newspaper war that resulted when Joseph Pulitzer and William Randolph Hearst both wanted *The Yellow Kid* for their newspapers. It was not long after this battle that people realized that comic strips could be sold to more than one paper at a time. Soon newspaper syndicates were formed, and that is how the comics are sold to newspapers around the world today. Somewhere on your favorite comic strip, though it may be too small to see clearly, is the name of the syndicate that distributes it to your newspaper.

Every author wants a publisher—a company that will print his or her books and sell them to bookstores and libraries, and every cartoonist wants to be syndicated. Syndication is a way of being certain that the cartoonist's art is distributed to as many people as possible. Literally hundreds of millions of people read a newspaper every day, and most read the funny pages.

When a cartoonist signs a contract with a syndicate, the syndicate acts as the author's sales agent. No other syndicate can represent the cartoonist during the length of the contract. The syndicate's sales force works hard to promote the cartoonist and to get more and more papers to subscribe to the comic strip. Newspapers pay a fee to the syndicate for the privilege of reprinting the comic strip or whatever other article, such as an advice column, that the syndicate is selling. The larger the newspaper's circulation, the bigger the fee the paper will have to pay in order to reprint the strip. The fees are then split between the cartoonist and the syndicate.

Each newspaper designs its own daily comic pages. This one is from the New York _Daily News_.

It is easy to sell familiar and popular strips and panels like _Dennis the Menace, Beetle Bailey,_ or _Peanuts,_ but it can be difficult to convince the comics editor of a newspaper to take a new and untried strip. As one newspaper editor, Ernie Williamson, says, "The new strips are pretty cheap, but they are a risk. No one knows whether the creator will be able to sustain the strip day in and day out."

The paper has a limited amount of space for the comic pages, and comic page editors choose carefully. In talking about how he selects comics for the _Houston Post,_ Mr. Williamson adds, "I try to look at the page as a whole. We don't want too many family strips and not enough adventure strips. After all, we want to appeal to kids, teenagers, and adults."

A newspaper will often survey its readers to see what comic strips they like and which ones they don't care for. Based on the results of the survey and the judgment of the editor of the comic pages, the newspaper will order the strips it wants.

As you can see, the syndicate does a lot of hard work for the cartoonists it represents. So how does a beginning cartoonist get syndicated? It isn't easy. "We get around five thousand submissions a year," says Sarah Gillespie of United Feature Syndicate. "They come from kids, prisoners, professional cartoonists—all kinds of people—and we look at all of them. But we only take about two to four new strips a year." King Features Syndicate receives around five thousand submissions each year, too, and Ted

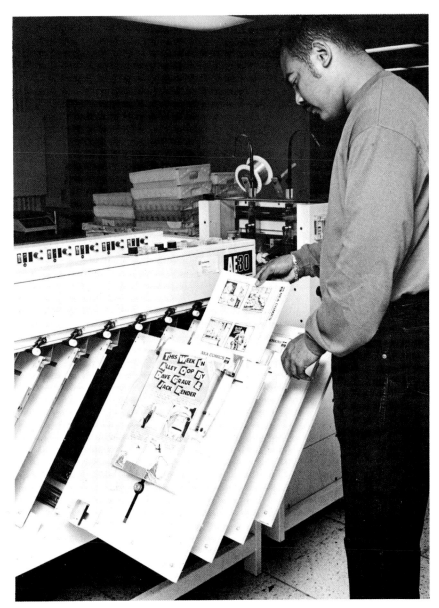

Special machines sort the comics that go to each subscribing newspaper.

Hannah says, "We may try three." And of the two, three, or four new strips that the syndicates try each year, one, or perhaps none, will become popular enough to be kept in syndication. It is hard to get syndicated, but it is even more difficult to stay syndicated.

So what are the cartoon editors at the syndicates looking for when they open their mail and read a new comic strip? Sarah Gillespie says, "We want to see at least six weeks of strips, and I'm looking for someone who draws well and writes funny, which are two different skills. If I find that person, I try to get to know them, to see if I think they can sustain a strip over the years."

Syndicates do a lot of work for the cartoonists they represent; here, an artist pastes down captions.

A new, untried cartoonist may be put under a development contract if the syndicate thinks the strip has potential. The development contract gives the syndicate an option. Its editors will work with the new cartoonist and try to help him or her bring the strip up to a publishable level. In exchange for this help, the cartoonist agrees not to try to sell the strip to another, competing syndicate. Once the strip is ready, the syndicate will promote it and try to sell it to as many newspapers as possible.

"A new comic strip is a fragile work of art," says Sarah Gillespie. "The first eighteen months are the roughest." It takes a while for a comic strip to catch on with its readers, but it doesn't have much time to accomplish that feat. And because the space on the comic pages is shrinking, when a newspaper agrees to take a new strip, it usually knocks another strip off the page in order to make room for the newcomer. "Cartoonists are supportive of one another's work," Ms. Gillespie says. "So it's hard." Then she adds, "However, if a comic strip survives the first three to five years, it will probably survive fifteen to twenty more."

For the fortunate cartoonists whose strips are surviving, getting published is a routine process. Their strips—six dailies and a Sunday—come into the syndicate in batches and are checked off on a tracking sheet as soon as they arrive. Cartoonists work eight to ten weeks ahead of publication, so the comics you read today arrived at their syndicates at least two months ago.

The strips then go to the editor, who checks the lettering

New strips get logged in at the syndicate as soon as they arrive.

and the art. If the Sunday strip has not been colored by the cartoonist, an artist at the syndicate will color it in according to the codes that are on the drawing.

Paul Hendricks is the senior comics editor at King Features, and he edits _Blondie_, among many other strips. "I check for spelling errors," Mr. Hendricks says. "And mistakes in the art. Once Blondie was drawn on the wrong side of the bed; another time the fish was left out of Dagwood's sandwich. We got thousands of letters! The fans watch for these things."

Sarah Gillespie says, "I was so nervous when I began editing Charles Schulz that I would stand up every time we talked on the phone. He heard about that, and one day he called and said, 'This is Sparky. Are you standing up?' "

Above: Occasionally an artist at the syndicate will color a cartoonist's Sunday strip.

Below: Sarah Gillespie is not standing up this time, as she chats on the phone and enjoys the new *Peanuts* strips.

The bit of teasing made Ms. Gillespie relax, and now she sits down when she has to talk to *Peanuts*'s creator. There isn't much editing that needs to be done with a cartoonist of Charles Schulz's stature. "Sometimes I have a question about spelling," Ms. Gillespie says. "He quotes the Bible a lot, but he doesn't use the King James Version. We didn't have a copy of the Revised Standard Version he uses here, so I called him once with a question about a word, and since he is a former Sunday School teacher, I got an explanation along with an answer!"

Newspapers usually buy comics from more than one syndicate. In addition to King Features and United Feature, there are various other syndicates scattered around the United States. The procedure for producing comic strips is similar in each one.

Once the syndicates receive their comics from the cartoonists and the strips have been edited, they are ready to be reproduced for the subscribing newspapers. The black-and-white strips, or dailies, are far easier to print than the Sunday color comics, so most syndicates handle the printing themselves. The original strips are far too large to be reproduced "as is" for newspapers, so special cameras in the production part of the syndicate photograph the strips and reduce them to the size needed for the newspapers. This process is similar to the way things can be reduced in size by a copying machine. The six daily strips are then printed on one piece of white paper suitable for reproduction. The comic strip is now "camera ready." If 1,600 newspapers have ordered *Peanuts*, then 1,600

A week's worth of daily strips are printed at one time.

Small printing presses produce the daily strips.

sheets will be printed. If only 500 papers ordered it, then 500 sheets would be printed.

This procedure is repeated for every comic strip and panel that the syndicate represents. Since each paper orders its comics individually, Paper A may get *Blondie*, *Dennis the Menace*, and *Beetle Bailey*, while Paper B wants *Blondie*, *Hi and Lois*, and *Crock*. There is a lot of sorting out and keeping up with orders, but computers make the job easier. The syndicates see to it that each paper receives the comic strips it has ordered.

Newspapers receive a week's worth of comic strips at a time, and these bundles arrive at the paper six weeks before the strips are to be run. If you look carefully at the comic strips and panels in your newspaper, you will see that the cartoonist has put a date somewhere on the art-

A week's worth of *Curtis* by Ray Billingsley.

work, indicating the day that strip or panel is to appear in the paper.

Someone at the newspaper then cuts the camera-ready strips apart. All of the strips are sorted by the day of the week. The strips are pasted onto a mat in the way the editor wants the finished comic page to look, and that board is photographed and printed along with the rest of the daily newspaper. This procedure is followed Monday through Saturday. The Sunday comics arrive in a much more complicated manner.

When they arrive at the newspaper, the comics are pasted into place.

Fiorello LaGuardia

7

SUNDAY FUNNIES

Most people's lives are very busy with school, work, and other activities. It is possible, then, that even the most devoted fan will occasionally miss reading his or her favorite comic strip during the week. But hardly anyone misses reading the Sunday funnies! In fact, in 1945, when there was a newspaper strike in New York City, the mayor, Fiorello LaGuardia, read the funnies aloud over the radio—with great dramatic expression. Mayor LaGuardia felt that no one should have to miss the Sunday comics just because newspaper employees and management could not agree on employment terms. Since the Yellow Kid made his appearance almost one hundred years ago, reading the Sunday comics has been and continues to be a weekend ritual for literally millions of readers around the world.

There are 170 different Sunday comic strips in the United States. In addition, Sunday funnies appear in papers from Istanbul to Calcutta to Buenos Aires. Practically all of these colored comic sections are prepared for the world's newspapers by the technicians and artists at American Color, a comic production facility.

Before the Sunday comics can be printed, the artwork has to go through a process called color separation. In order to understand how color separation works, you need to know that any printing facility deals with only four basic colors—black, a special shade of red called magenta, yellow, and a special shade of blue called cyan. Printers

The Sunday comics roll off the printing press.

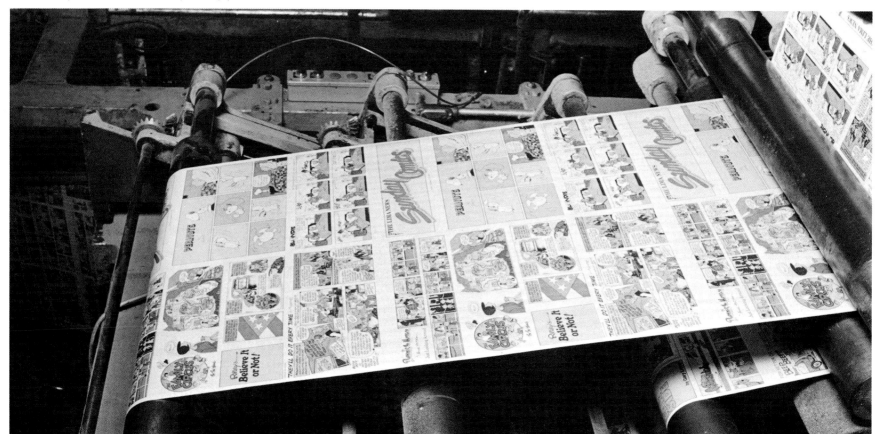

use magenta and cyan instead of any other shades of red and blue because these two shades mix particularly well with other colors. But wait, you may think. If the printer only works with red, blue, black, and yellow, why are the comics full of all kinds of colors—purple, pink, green, brown? The answer is, the four basic colors are combined to produce new colors.

You have probably painted with watercolors from time to time, and you know that a combination of red and blue will make purple, and yellow and blue together turn into green, while mixing red, yellow, and blue together will give you brown.

Printed material is colored by a kind of "mixing together," too. However, since the newspapers are not working with paint, the mixing is done in layers. One color is laid on top of another color in order to create a third color. This process is not done with a brush, but with a computer.

When the Sunday comics arrive from their different syndicates, someone at American Color will log them in. American Color keeps track of the comics, just as the syndicates do. They know when a strip should arrive, and they know if it is late.

People will check the art to be certain all the areas have been colored and coded with the proper number from the printer's chart. They will make sure the black outlines of the figures and the lettering in the balloons are sharp and clear. When they are satisfied that the strip is camera ready, it goes to the next step in the process. A special camera will photograph the strip and make a master negative that preserves all the details in the original art. That negative is used to make a black-and-white print of the comic strip, and is used later in the printing process as well.

The next step is done by hand. Someone goes over the now black-and-white comic strip and removes everything but the most essential black lines. The words in the balloons are whited out, and all the extra details in the art are taken away. What is left is a simple outline of the strip.

That simplified comic strip is put on a drum, and a laser beam "reads" the comic and stores the image in a com-

At American Color, an editor uses a computer to separate the colors in the comic strip.

puter. Now the comic strip is ready to receive its color, and a computer (run by a human color editor) does much of the work.

Using a monitor and a computer mouse, the color editor moves the cursor over the strip, coloring in the shades the cartoonist has indicated. It's a bit like doing a coloring book with a computer. The monitor shows the editor how he or she is doing with the coloring. Michelle Kushnirik is a color editor working for American Color. She says, "We used to do this work by hand. It's a whole lot easier now!" Working by hand, it would take one person eight hours to color separate a comic strip. Depending on the detail in the artwork, most Sunday funnies can be separated in an hour to an hour and a half. It may take longer, if the art is more complicated. Ms. Kushnirik says, "*Prince Valiant* may take three hours to do, but I can do *Peanuts* in one." This process of color separation is done for each individual strip.

When the color editor is finished coloring the comic, the computer will output a negative for each basic color—magenta, yellow, and cyan. The master negative is used for the color black.

Each newspaper has a certain way it wants its Sunday comic section to look. The look of a page is called the layout, and the people at American Color know the layout that each newspaper wants for its comic section. Using the four negatives for each strip, they make prints of each comic strip and paste up four full-page layouts of the comic page for each newspaper. These pages are shot by

Above: Prints of the Sunday comics get pasted into place.

Below: Each comic page is photographed and a negative for each color is produced.

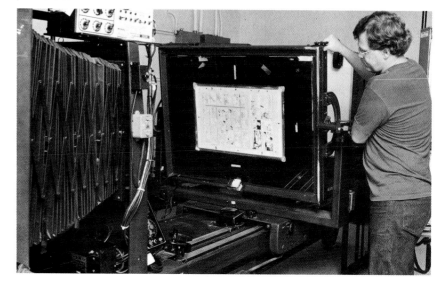

another camera in order to get another negative of the full page, with all the strips in their proper places. The full-page negatives of all four colors are now ready to be turned into printing plates.

In photo negatives, the colors are reversed. Things that are black in the negative are white in the printed photo, and vice versa. You could say that the snapshot is a positive of the negative. It is that way with comic strip negatives, too. When that negative is "developed," it will produce a positive image that is the printing plate.

To make a printing plate, a special kind of liquid plastic sensitive to ultraviolet light is placed on a metal plate that is thicker than tinfoil but thinner than a cookie sheet. The negative goes on top of this plate. Next, ultraviolet light shines on the negative. The light pierces the clear parts of the negative and begins a chemical reaction in the plastic, hardening it where the light hits it. The light can't get through the dark parts of the negative, so that plastic will not get hardened. In fact, the liquid plastic will get washed away, so only a raised picture for the comic strip will remain on the printing plate. For color comics, there will be four plates made—one for red (magenta), blue (cyan), yellow, and black. The plates are sent to the printer and put on a giant printing press.

Each negative is carefully checked before it is sent to platemaking.

A platemaking machine turns the negative into a printing plate.

The Sunday funnies are printed in four stages, using the four different color plates. The colors are mixed by using dots of ink. The smaller the dot, the lighter the color. For example, the same blue ink—cyan—is used to create all shades of blue. If a light blue is needed, the dots of ink are small. More of the plain white of the newsprint shows, and the human eye "mixes" the tiny blue dot with the white paper and "sees" light blue. If a darker blue was needed, the blue dots would be bigger. Then less "white" background would show, and our eyes would be tricked into thinking we saw dark blue. That is exactly how other colors are created, too. Red dots laid over blue dots will make you think you "see" purple. Your eye has been fooled, for what you are really seeing are two separate colors. If you look carefully at the Sunday funnies, you will be able to see these dots, results of the "mixing," and you will begin to understand how color separation works.

When the comic pages are finally printed, American Color ships them off to the subscribing newspapers. The newspapers then insert the comics into their Sunday editions, and everyone across the country enjoys them.

This page: Giant machines automatically fold the funnies.

Facing page: Sunday comics, hot off the press *(left)*. A pressman periodically checks the run for quality *(top right)*. Neatly stacked on skids, the comics are ready to be shipped to the newspapers *(bottom right)*.

COMIC BOOKS
FOR FUN AND PROFIT

No discussion of funny papers would be complete without talking about comic books. Chances are, your parents and grandparents had stacks of comic books when they were young. Perhaps you have a stack of your own right now.

Technically, the comic book began in 1911 when the popular *Mutt and Jeff* strips were gathered into book form and published. However, it was another twenty-two years before the comic book as we know it today really got started.

In 1933, two high school students, Jerry Siegel and Joe Shuster, became interested in a kind of writing called science fiction. They decided to put out their own magazine, which they produced by using their school's mimeograph machine. Jerry Siegel wrote stories about a superhero who could "hurdle skyscrapers . . . leap an eighth of a mile . . . raise tremendous weights . . . run faster than a stream-lined train . . . and nothing less than a bursting shell could penetrate his skin! Joe Shuster illustrated the character doing all of these things . . . and more. Siegel and Shuster called their stories "Reign of the Superman," and though the boys could not have known it at the time, they had created an American legend.

DC Comics was a relatively new comic book publishing company in 1938. In addition to publishing *Detective Comics*, DC decided to introduce another comic book in June of 1938. The new comic book was called *Action Comics*, and for $130, the publishers bought the rights to the Superman character from Jerry Siegel and Joe Shuster. The rest, as people say, is history. The Superman stories took the country by storm, and other comics with other superheroes soon followed.

Superman appeared as a comic book in 1938; by 1940, there were 60 new comic books on the newsstands of America. By 1941, there were 108 more, featuring the exploits of heroes with names such as Batman, Captain Marvel, Wonder Woman, Sub-Mariner, Flash Gordon, and Buck Rogers.

The world was a troubled place when *Superman* first appeared. Adolph Hitler's armies were on the march in Europe, and though the United States was not yet involved in the fighting, it was watching Nazi Germany with an anxious eye. Like the comic strips, the comic books began to reflect what was going on in American life. The

Captain America

United States officially entered World War II in December 1941, but by then, comic book heroes had been fighting the enemy for nearly two years. In fact, in February 1940, the Sub-Mariner was fighting Nazis on the cover of a Marvel comic book. The war progressed, and America's young men and women joined the armed forces. As patriotism filled the land, new comic books appeared with titles such as *Wings, Our Flag, The Eagle,* and *Captain America.* As their names indicate, all of these comics dealt with patriotic themes, as America struggled in World War II.

Of course, the main purpose of the comics has always been entertainment. War or not, people still wanted to laugh. In addition to the funny papers, new comic books appeared that helped readers do just that. Many of the characters in the new comic books were already famous from movie cartoons; others appeared for the first time in comic books, and only later became "stars" in movie theaters and on television. Mickey Mouse and Donald Duck were already popular when they appeared in comic book form. On the other hand, Archie Andrews and his friends Jughead, Veronica, Reggie, and Betty were created as comic book characters, and had their own animated television show much later.

Comic books enjoyed great popularity during the 1940s. They cost ten cents, and practically every child in America had several of them that they read, reread, then traded with their friends. In time, however, comic books began to change. Gradually, a new kind of title appeared on the newsstands. *Donald Duck* and *Superman* were still popular, but kids were also reading comics with titles such as *Tales from the Crypt*, *Worlds of Fear*, and *Adventures into Terror*.

Ever since there have been parents and children, people have worried about children's behavior. In 1954, a subcommittee from the United States Senate held a hearing in New York City. The subject was juvenile delinquency, and the senators wanted to find out if some of America's comic books—especially the ones with horror and violence in them—were turning children into juvenile delin-

Comic books can be read in any position.

quents. A prominent psychiatrist and author, Dr. Frederic Wertham, had written a book called *Seduction of the Innocent*. In the book, Dr. Wertham implied that comic books were contributing to juvenile delinquency in America. He appeared before the Senate subcommittee and testified that, in his opinion, comic books were bad for children. Suddenly, everyone was worried about comic books. Newspapers published editorials against them, and parents refused to let their children buy them. There were even comic book burnings!

In September 1954, in order to preserve their business,

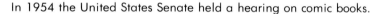

In 1954 the United States Senate held a hearing on comic books.

comic book publishers formed an organization called the Comics Magazine Association of America. On a voluntary basis, each publisher submitted copies of each new comic book, along with its advertising, to a committee from this organization. The committee reviewed each comic book, and if it was approved, it received the Comics Authority Code seal. Parents looked for this seal. If a comic book did not have it, it usually did not get purchased. Once again, the opinions and feelings of the American people were reflected in the comic books. Though the seal does not appear on comic books today, most comic book publishers adhere to standards that were set during the time the committee was in existence.

Fortunately, even though they were criticized, comic books as a whole never went out of business. Instead, they grew. Today there are at least thirteen major comic book publishers, who, among them, create well over 250 comic books each month.

Marvel Comics is the largest comic book publisher in the United States. It publishes more than one hundred comic books each month, but none is more popular than *The Amazing Spider-Man*, created by Stan Lee. Stan Lee began his comic book career as a teenager. In 1940, he joined Marvel Comics. During his long career, he has been head writer, art director, and editor in chief, and now he is the publisher. Despite the responsibilities that Mr. Lee has, he still writes the daily comic strip, *The Amazing Spider-Man*, though others may write the adventures that appear in the comic books.

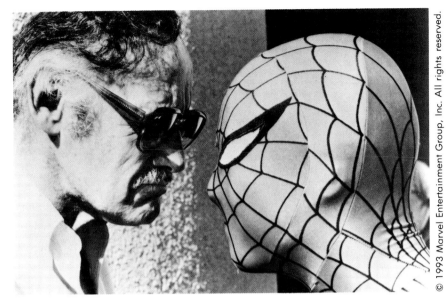

A face-off between the creator and his creature—Stan Lee and Spider-Man.

Spider-Man made his first appearance in August 1962 in a Marvel Comic called *Amazing Fantasy*. Poor Spidey, as he is affectionately called, almost didn't make it as a cartoon character, because some people at *Amazing Fantasy* thought that stories about a spider would be distasteful and because *Amazing Fantasy* was not a popular comic book. Stan Lee decided to put his new superhero on the cover, anyway. "Nobody cares what you put in a book that's going to die, so I threw in Spider-Man," Stan Lee has said. "I featured him on the cover and then forgot about him."

Stan Lee might have forgotten his new character, but the readers did not. Spider-Man did not die. Instead, sales of *Amazing Fantasy* jumped, and in less than a year *The Amazing Spider-Man* had his own comic book. Today *The Amazing Spider-Man* still appears in comic books, as well as in daily comic strips. He fights off villains and fights for literacy, as you can see from the illustration from a special Spider-Man comic on this page.

The Amazing Spider-Man

When he appeared, Spidey was different from traditional comic book superheroes like Superman. Spider-Man had doubts, worries, even fears. The "humanizing" influence of Spider-Man eventually affected other superheroes. Even Superman changed from the Man of Steel to a hero who could cry, and bleed, and even die! In late 1992, DC Comics announced that Superman would be killed at the hands of a character named Doomsday. The news caused as much commotion and comment in America's newspapers and on television news shows as Blondie's job had done. On October 4, 1992, the prestigious *New York Times* ran an editorial commenting on the Man of Steel's death. The writer ended the piece by noting, "Doubtlessly, DC Comics will see to it that Superman is subsequently born again; he's too big a part of the business to stay dead." Actually, in 1993, *four* Supermen returned, in four separate issues of the comic book, teasing readers with new questions about his identity.

Unlike comic strips, which rely on a syndicate to get them into readers' hands, the comic book is published by a company. At Marvel, as at all publishers, the story comes first. Creating the story is often a group effort by the editor, the writer, and the artist. Those three people meet together to discuss story ideas. Then the writer produces an outline of the story and sends it on to the artist, or penciler, as that person is called in the comic book business. The penciler draws a rough draft of each page of the comic book, based on the writer's outline. This rough draft is called a storyboard. As in a comic strip, the action takes place in panels and the dialogue is in balloons—but the balloons are left empty at this point.

When everyone—the editor, the artist, and the writer—is satisfied with the storyboards for each page, the pages go back to the writer to decide on the exact words for the

Spider-Man's adventures are popular and exciting reading.

balloons. Next comes a rough pencil dummy to show the page layout; then a final pencil drawing of each page is made. A photostat, or photographic copy, is made of that pencil drawing, and the pages are then ready for the next step—inking. Ink artists carefully go over the pencil artist's work, using permanent black ink; then the pages go to a letterer, who inserts the dialogue in the balloons.

Comic books begin with a story outline and a rough pencil sketch.

The final pencil drawing goes to an inker.

Pencilers do a final drawing of the rough sketch.

79

After the picture is inked, the story is lettered in balloons.

The cover and interior pages are hand-colored by an artist.

Finally, the pages are ready to be colored, and there is a separate artist, called a colorer, to do that work. The art for the cover is painted, and the comic is ready to go to a production facility to be printed.

Traditionally, comic books have been inexpensive reading material. The first ones cost ten cents each. Today's comics still cost far less than a paperback book. In order to keep the cost down, comic books are printed on inexpensive paper, and they have soft covers. Even though today's comic books are far better in quality than the first ones were, they are still easily ruined. Through the years, millions of copies of comic books have been thrown away—because they became tattered and torn, or because someone grew up and got tired of his collection.

Some people, however, saved their comic books, putting them in boxes and trunks and lugging them up to attics. Between 1937 and 1953, Edgar Church, who lived in Colorado, collected comic books. He stored them in eight-foot-high stacks in a dark room. The climate in Colorado is dry, which is perfect for preserving paper, and Edgar Church's comic book collection was perfectly preserved. Today each comic book in the Church collection looks as if it was just brought home from the newsstand.

Comic book collecting has always been a hobby, but now it is big business. There are conventions all across the country where people come to look at comic books, buy, sell, and trade them. A comic from the Edgar Church collection is the most expensive kind of comic a collector

Sotheby's prints an elegant catalog of the comics it plans to sell at auction.

A comic-book collector checks a current price guide.

can own. In December 1991, Sotheby's, an internationally famous auction house, held an auction of comic books and comic art. An April 1937 ten-cent copy of *Detective Comics* that was in Edgar Church's collection sold for $16,500. The May 1939 issue of *Detective Comics* has on its cover: "Starting this issue: the amazing and unique adventures of THE BATMAN!" That comic was not part of the Edgar Church collection, but it was in very fine condition, and it sold for $55,000 at the same auction. In all, $1,205,905 of comic books and comic art was sold that day. Comic art may not hang on the walls of our most famous museums, but collectors are aware of its value. Today comic books are collected for fun *and* for profit.

OF RINGS
AND THINGS...

Everyone is used to seeing the faces of Snoopy, Blondie, Spider-Man, and Garfield in the comic pages. However, their famous faces, along with many others, also appear on lunch boxes, toothbrushes, dolls, stuffed animals, pajamas, slippers, pencils, greeting cards, notepaper—the list goes on and on. There are literally hundreds of products that bear the image of famous comic characters.

When a person creates something, whether it is a manuscript, a painting, or a musical composition, the creative work is often protected by copyright. When something is copyrighted, no one other than the person or company in whose name the material is copyrighted can use it. Comic strips are protected by copyright, too. Sometimes the cartoonist holds the copyright to the characters, and sometimes the syndicate does. No one is allowed to publish drawings of comic characters, or reprint comic strips, without getting permission from the cartoonist or the syndicate. For example, the comic strip *Nancy* was created by Ernie Bushmiller. When he died, the strip stopped for a while. Then, because United Feature owned the rights to *Nancy*, they asked Jerry Scott to begin drawing it again. However, Jerry Scott, or even a member of Ernie Bushmiller's family, could not have drawn the new *Nancy* without permission from United Feature.

Copyrights protect everyone. Sarah Gillespie says, "I represent the cartoonist's interests, so I will remind a newspaper that reproduces Garfield or Snoopy without our permission, that it cannot do that. Newspapers are our clients and we want to be helpful, but we have to keep

Real Life Adventures

Real Life Adventures
© 1992 Garlan Co.
Reprinted with permission
Universal Press Syndicate.
All rights reserved.

Suction-cup animals, like many things, are best in moderation.

quality control going." A poor reproduction of Snoopy or Garfield does not do justice to the careful art of Charles Schulz or Jim Davis.

The copyright also prevents anyone from reproducing Snoopy, Garfield, Blondie, Popeye or any character on toys, dishes, or clothing, in an advertisement, or on anything at all without getting permission and paying a fee. The fee is called a licensing fee, because a license is a way of giving people permission to do things. A driver's license gives people permission to drive; a license from United Feature Syndicate gives a company permission to make stuffed Garfields with suction cups on their feet. However, any cartoon character that is reproduced under a licensing agreement must be approved by the syndicate before manufacturing can begin. The Snoopys, Blondies, and Garfields on lunch boxes and sheets must be up to the artistic standard of the *real* Snoopy, Blondie, or Garfield that appears in the funny papers.

Of course, the syndicates and the cartoonists like to license their characters to manufacturers. The manufacturers pay a fee, and the cartoon character gets a lot of publicity, which increases the number of people who read the comic strip. And some of these characters, such as Snoopy and Garfield, have made their creators very wealthy. Thanks to licensing agreements, Charles Schulz is one of the ten wealthiest people in show business, earning more than celebrities like Madonna, Garth Brooks, Prince, and Arnold Schwarzenegger, to name just a few.

If a manufacturer has paid a licensing fee, the characters

Stuffed Snoopys come in many sizes.

may appear many times over. However, sometimes people are given permission to reproduce a comic strip character, or the strip itself, one time only. The comic strips in this book are authorized to be reproduced just for this book. The author and publisher cannot reproduce them again in any other kind of work.

Products that you can hold in your hand are not the only ways comic strips live away from their newspapers. From the earliest days of the comics, there have been Broadway plays, radio and television shows, and Hollywood movies featuring comic characters. Li'l Abner, Charlie Brown, Popeye, and Superman have all had Broadway productions written about them. Dick Tracy, Little Orphan Annie, and Buck Rogers, among others, starred on

PEANUTS Characters 1951, 1952, 1958, 1965 United Feature Syndicate, Inc.

"You're A Good Man, Charlie Brown"

A MUSICAL ENTERTAINMENT FOR THE ENTIRE FAMILY
BASED ON THE COMIC STRIP "PEANUTS" BY CHARLES M. SCHULZ
MUSIC AND LYRICS BY CLARK GESNER

85

the radio, and when television became popular, still more comic strips were adapted for the small screen. Some were animated cartoons, and others, like "Dennis the Menace," had human actors playing the roles. Comic strips went to Hollywood, and films like *Dick Tracy, Batman*, and a feature-length *Dennis the Menace* were the result.

Comic strips and their characters have also been turned into fine art, the kind that hangs in museums and art galleries. Roy Lichtenstein is an artist who paints canvases that look like comic strips. In talking about his work, he says, "I was serious about the comic strips, yet I also expected them to look funny, because the whole idea of doing a comic strip is humorous."

Roy Lichtenstein is right. The idea of doing a comic strip is humorous, but as you have seen, there is a serious side to the funny papers, too. From their beginnings almost one hundred years ago, the comics have allowed others to know what life in America is like and, at the same time, have allowed Americans to laugh, and talk, and get to know one another better. Like any good piece of literature, the funny papers let us see the world from another viewpoint—as the cartoonist sees it. We may agree or disagree with this view. We may like some strips and not like others, but no matter how we feel about the strips, one thing about them is true. Comic strips, books, and panels are art forms that were born in this country, continue to grow here, and are shared with and enjoyed by people scattered all over the world. Our funny papers are a part of the heritage of every American. We should be proud of them.

Reading the funny papers is an American tradition.

AFTERWORD

Most professions have organizations that support their members by holding conventions, where members get together to share ideas and information and enjoy one another's company. The professional organization for cartoonists is the National Cartoonists Society. Every year this organization presents awards for excellence at its annual convention, which is held in a different city around the country each year. The awards are similar to the Oscars and the Emmys because cartoonists can win in a number of categories—newspaper comic strip, newspaper panel, animation, comic books, sports cartoons, and editorial cartoons, to name a few. However, the major award is Outstanding Cartoonist of the Year. Each award is called a Reuben, named after the cartoonist Rube Goldberg, who designed it and was the first president of the National Cartoonists Society. An editorial cartoonist, Bill Crawford, made the first Reuben out of bronze. The Reuben for Outstanding Cartoonist of the Year has been awarded at the National Cartoonists Society convention every year since its beginning in 1946.

OUTSTANDING CARTOONIST OF THE YEAR

1946	Milton Caniff	_Steve Canyon_	1969	Walter Berndt	_Smitty_
1947	Al Capp	_Li'l Abner_	1970	Alfred Andriola	_Kerry Drake_
1948	Chic Young	_Blondie_	1971	Milton Caniff	_Steve Canyon_
1949	Alex Raymond	_Rip Kirby_	1972	Pat Oliphant	_Editorial_
1950	Roy Crane	_Buz Sawyer_	1973	Dik Browne	_Hagar the Horrible_
1951	Walt Kelly	_Pogo_	1974	Dick Moores	_Gasoline Alley_
1952	Hank Ketcham	_Dennis the Menace_	1975	Bob Dunn	_They'll Do It Every Time_
1953	Mort Walker	_Beetle Bailey_	1976	Ernie Bushmiller	_Nancy_
1954	Willard Mullin	_Sports_	1977	Chester Gould	_Dick Tracy_
1955	Charles Schulz	_Peanuts_	1978	Jeff MacNelly	_Editorial_
1956	Herbert L. Block	_Editorial_	1979	Jeff MacNelly	_Shoe_
1957	Hal Foster	_Prince Valiant_	1980	Charles Saxon	_Advertising_
1958	Frank King	_Gasoline Alley_	1981	Mell Lazarus	_Miss Peach_ and _Momma_
1959	Chester Gould	_Dick Tracy_	1982	Bil Keane	_Family Circus_
1960	Ronald Searle	_Advertising & Illustration_	1983	Arnold Roth	_Advertising_
1961	Bill Mauldin	_Editorial_	1984	Brant Parker	_The Wizard of Id_
1962	Dik Browne	_Hi and Lois_	1985	Lynn Johnston	_For Better or For Worse_
1963	Fred Laswell	_Barney Google and Snuffy Smith_	1986	Bill Watterson	_Calvin and Hobbes_
1964	Charles Schulz	_Peanuts_	1987	Mort Drucker	_Mad Magazine_
1965	Leonard Starr	_On Stage_	1988	Bill Watterson	_Calvin and Hobbes_
1966	Otto Soglow	_The Little King_	1989	Jim Davis	_Garfield_
1967	Rube Goldberg	_Humor in Sculpture_	1990	Gary Larson	_The Far Side_
1968	Pat Oliphant	_Editorial_	1991	Mike Peters	_Mother Goose & Grimm_
	Johnny Hart	_B.C._ and _The Wizard of Id_	1992	Cathy Guisewite	_Cathy_

INDEX